KINGS ✦ AND ✦ QUEENS

William I

Richard Wood

Wayland

Titles in the series

Elizabeth I
Henry VIII
James VI/I
Mary Queen of Scots
Queen Victoria
William I

Series editor: Sarah Doughty
Book editor: Katie Orchard
Consultant: Dr Andy Orchard
Designer: Jean Wheeler
Production controller: Carol Stevens

First published in 1995 by Wayland (Publishers) Ltd
61 Western Road, Hove, East Sussex, BN3 1JD, England

British Library Cataloguing in Publication Data
Wood, Richard
William I – (Kings and Queens series)
I. Title II. Series
942.021092

ISBN 0 7502 1452 X

Typeset by Jean Wheeler
Printed and bound in Italy by Rotolito Lombarda S.p.A.

Cover: A sixteenth-century portrait of William I. Artist unknown.

Picture acknowledgements:
Ancient Art & Architecture Collection 5 (bottom), 9 (both), 29 (left); Bodleian Library, Oxford 15 (MS. LAUD. MISC. 636.58R) bottom, 25 (MS BODL. 569. fol 1R) top; Bridgeman Art Library *cover* (Philip Mould Historical Portraits Ltd.), *title page* (British Library), 6–7 (Giraudon), 7 (British Library) bottom, 11 (British Library) top, 16 (British Library), 18 (British Library) bottom, 20 (Philip Mould Historical Portraits Ltd.), 23 (British Museum) bottom, 27 (John Bethell) top; Corporation of London Records Office 15 (top); E. T. Archive 24, 28; Mary Evans 8; Forest Life Picture Library 21 (bottom); Robert Harding 13 (both), 14 (bottom), 17, 18 (top), 19, 23 (top), 25 (bottom), 27 (bottom), 29 (right); Michael Holford 5 (top), 10, 11 (bottom), 12, 14 (top), 21 (top); Angelo Hornak 22; Richard Wood 26.
Artwork on page 4 is supplied by Hard Lines.

Contents

A Troubled Youth

On a battlefield in Hastings in 1066, the Normans charged at the English on their horses, and trampled them into the ground. The battle was for the throne of England, and the price for losing was death. By evening, King Harold of England lay dead. William, **Duke** of Normandy became William I of England (William the Conqueror), and history was made. Who would have thought that this Norman invader would become one of the most powerful kings of his day?

A map showing England and Normandy in 1066.

William's birthplace at Falaise, Normandy. The castle was rebuilt not long after his death in 1087.

This powerful king did not have a very remarkable start in life. Born in 1027, he was the **illegitimate** son of Herleva, a **tanner's** daughter from the small town of Falaise in Normandy. William's father was Robert, the duke or ruler of that part of France. Robert never married Herleva because he was unable to marry a woman of such low **status**. He did, however, remain faithful to her.

We know very little else about William's birth and childhood. Many **legends** about his birth were written down in the next century, when people already knew about William's later life. We do know that it was unlikely that William would become duke because he was illegitimate, and one of his older relatives would have claimed the title. But Duke Robert had William brought up in his own household to prepare him to be the next duke.

A nineteenth-century statue of William's grandfather. He ruled Normandy between 942–96.

The Normans were a warlike people who were very skilled horsemen. This picture shows part of the Bayeux Tapestry, which was woven in about 1077. It explained why and how William invaded England in 1066.

William's **ancestors** were **Viking** raiders from Scandinavia who settled in France during the ninth century. In 911, the King of France gave their leader, Rollo, the right to rule part of his kingdom. Rollo called it Normandy – the land of the North Men. It was a difficult land to rule. Many warlike families were trying to seize wealth for themselves. However, Rollo's **descendants** kept power, and William's father, Robert, became Duke in 1027.

To hold power, the duke needed the support of the Church. In 1035, Robert set out on a pilgrimage to Jerusalem. He hoped to win favour with God and the Church. He knew that it was a risky journey. Before he left, Robert told his lords that, if he died, William was to be the next duke. They swore a solemn **oath** to support William. Robert then set out for the Holy Land. When the news of his death reached Normandy, William became Duke. Despite their promises, the Norman lords soon began to fight each

other once more. William's steward and guardians, Count Gilbert of Brionne and Count Alan of Brittany, were murdered, and his own life was often in danger.

William never learned how to read or write. But he developed a strong faith in God and a keen sense of right and wrong. His early lessons in riding, hunting and fighting made him brave and strong. By the time he was twenty, he was ready to take command of Normandy for himself.

From boyhood, William's favourite sport was hunting. This later illustration shows him riding with hounds.

A Most Glorious Duke

William realized that he must control the Norman lords if he was ever to rule his lands properly. His chance came in 1047, when his cousin, Guy of Brionne, claimed the right to be Duke of Normandy. William acted swiftly. He collected some supporters and then persuaded King Henry of France (1031–1060) to send an army to help him. At Val-ès-Dunes, they fought a fierce battle. Eventually, William's supporters pushed back the **rebel** forces until they drowned in the River Orne.

The ruins of the castle at Arques, from a nineteenth-century illustration. In 1053, William's army surrounded the castle and forced his rebellious uncle William to surrender it to him.

William now turned his attention to enemies on the borders of Normandy, such as Count Geoffrey of Anjou, who ruled lands to the south of Normandy. His troops made frequent raids on William's **territory**. In 1052, William decided to punish Geoffrey, and captured his castles at Alençon and Domfront.

William's soldiers were impressed by his great energy as he led his army, tirelessly encouraging them. His bravery became a legend when, with just fifty soldiers, he beat off an enemy attack by 300 men. But William's cruelty also inspired fear. Some townspeople in Alençon mocked William by beating skins to remind him of his mother's humble family. As punishment, he had their hands and feet cut off. The people of Domfront quickly surrendered when they heard this. In 1057, King Henry turned against William, and Henry's troops were defeated in the Battle of Varaville.

(Above) La Trinité church, Caen, Normandy. In 1058, William's wife Matilda founded this convent for nuns to thank God for her marriage.

(Below) Norman soldiers were well protected with chainmail armour. This twelfth-century picture was painted on the wall of a chapel in France.

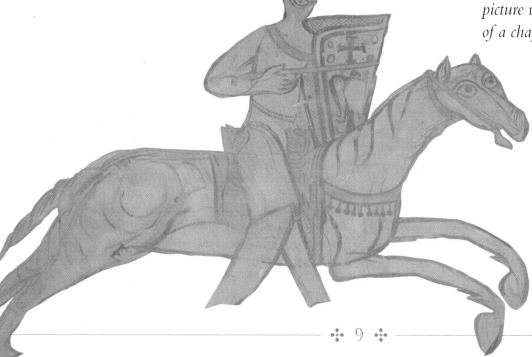

Count Geoffrey never forgave William for his attacks. Twice he invaded Normandy, but both times he was defeated. In 1060, Count Geoffrey died and so did King Henry. With no real challenge to his power, William now began to think of extending his own territories. His **conquests**, first of Maine and then of Brittany, left Normandy circled by friendly powers. They also gave William a chance to try out the methods he would later use to conquer and govern a greater prize – England.

Here, Harold touches holy relics while making a solemn promise to support William as king. When he broke his promise, William invaded.

William was distantly related to most of the English royal family through his great-aunt Emma. Emma had married two English kings in turn and was the mother of two more, including the reigning King Edward the Confessor (1042–1066). But Edward had no children. In 1051, he promised William that he would be the next king.

King Edward the Confessor. This illustration from a fourteenth-century law book shows the king at a feast.

William was not the only one with his eyes on the English crown. Harold, the Earl of Wessex and King Edward's brother-in-law, was favoured by many English lords. But in 1064, Harold was taken prisoner in France, and was passed over to William. In return for his freedom, Harold swore to support William as the next king. In January 1066, King Edward died. Instead of accepting William, the English lords immediately **elected** Harold, who was crowned in Westminster Abbey the next day. William decided to invade England and become king by conquest.

Preparations for conquest, from the Bayeux Tapestry. There are swords, spears and axes, suits of chainmail and helmets.

The Conquest of England

William could not invade England immediately in January. It was midwinter and his army was not ready. He needed ships, arms and armour. William had to raise money and win support, so he rode around Normandy and France, persuading people to join his army. In return, he promised them land and wealth once England was his. He told people how Harold had broken his oath, and even the **Pope** sent a banner to show his support.

William's fast longships took only a few hours to cross the Channel. Their shallow hulls enabled them to land horses and men directly on to the beach.

By September, the army was ready. William moved his **fleet** to the east to cross the English Channel by the shortest route. Weapons, horses and 7,000 men were loaded on to the new ships. They landed at Pevensey, near Hastings, on 28 September 1066. It is said that William fell on the beach and picked up a handful of sand to show that he would soon grasp the whole land.

IMPORTANT DATES

1066

6 January	Harold is crowned King.
15 August	William's fleet gathers at Dives, Normandy.
20 September	Norwegian troops invade northern England.
25 September	Harold's army defeats Norwegians at the Battle of Stamford Bridge.
27 September	William's fleet sails towards England.
1 October	Harold's army marches south.
14 October	William wins the Battle of Hastings.
25 December	William is crowned King.

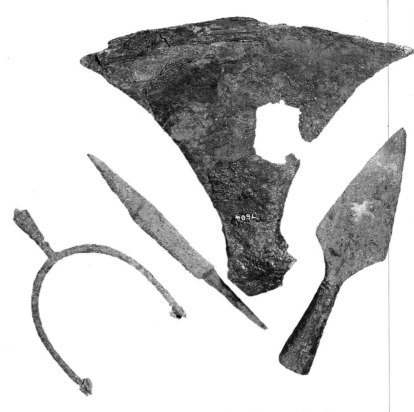

(Above) A spur, dagger, axe head and spear head. Both armies used weapons like these at the Battle of Hastings.

Harold's English army had patrolled the coast for months, but was nowhere to be seen. It had been forced to march to Yorkshire to defeat an army led by King Harald Hardrada of Norway, who also wanted the English throne. The news of William's invasion was brought to Harold in York, and he immediately went south again. After a march of 500 kilometres, his army arrived near Hastings on 14 October, exhausted and badly prepared for battle.

A Norman cavalry charge. Medieval battles were very cruel to horses as well as to men.

Harold's men took up position on a ridge of land called Senlac Hill. With no **cavalry** and few **archers**, they relied on close fighting with heavy swords to break up the Norman ranks.

The Normans were rested and ready for battle. Skilled archers and highly-trained horsemen managed to spread panic and confusion. At one point, a rumour spread that William was dead, and some Normans began to retreat. William bravely lifted his helmet to prove that he was still alive. Later, some Normans pretended to retreat. Harold's men ran down the hill in pursuit, only to be cut down when the Normans rounded on them from behind. By evening, Harold lay dead. His troops had fled. William had won the Battle of Hastings, one of the most important battles in English history.

The death of Harold, from the Bayeux Tapestry. The king appears to have an arrow in his eye here, but another picture shows him being stabbed with a sword. We do not know exactly how he died.

The building of the Tower of London was begun in 1067. It was one of the first and strongest royal castles in England.

(Left) This document is William's Charter along with his seal. It promises freedom for the people of London.

The English lords still would not accept William as king. Instead, they chose the fourteen-year-old Edgar Atheling, an Anglo-Saxon prince. But he was never crowned. After allowing his army to rest, William began a slow march towards London. He captured and burned Dover and Southwark as a warning against any towns trying to defy him. Other towns soon surrendered. On Christmas Day in 1066, William was crowned king in Westminster Abbey. The Normans cheered so loudly that the English people began to panic. Most of the **congregation** rushed out and the service was finished by the priests alone.

The Anglo-Saxon Chronicle, an important record of events written at the time. This page describes the years 1066–1068. The dates are in red on the left.

Securing the Kingdom

For almost ten years after the Battle of Hastings, William had to be on his guard against English rebels. If English lords did not accept William, he handed their lands over to his faithful Norman and French followers. In return, they promised to send soldiers to fight in his army when needed. Gradually, William also replaced the Church leaders with foreign churchmen. Like all medieval rulers, William needed the Church's support.

In March 1067, William returned to Normandy, leaving the government of England in the hands of his

Peasants harvesting wheat, from a fourteenth-century book. William's troops punished the northern rebels by burning their crops, farms and homes.

Bayeux Cathedral, Normandy. This church was rebuilt by Bishop Odo, William's half-brother, and is where the Bayeux Tapestry originally hung.

half-brother Odo and a Norman lord called William FitzOsbern. With William abroad, revolts broke out in Dover, then in Hereford and the West Country. Further north, the powerful English earls, Edwin and Morcar, also rose against William. By December, the king returned, leading his army against the rebels.

In 1069, a more serious revolt broke out in the north, led by Edgar Atheling. Supported by a Danish army, the rebels captured York and murdered its Norman governor. William marched his army across northern England. They burned homes, farms and crops, killing the animals and murdering the people they found. William's brutal methods worked. There were no further rebellions in the north. To prevent trouble from the Scots, William gave lands to King Malcolm of Scotland and made peace with him at Abernethy in 1072.

IMPORTANT DATES

1067 *William is in Normandy from March to December.*

1069–70 *Risings in Yorkshire and Durham are cruelly put down.*

1070 *William's friend, Lanfranc, becomes Archbishop of Canterbury.*

1071 *Hereward the Wake rebels against William.*

1072 *Peace of Abernethy signed with Scotland.*

(Right) Ely, the town where Hereward the Wake held out against William's troops. The town is perched on an island of high ground above the surrounding marshes. Later, Normans rebuilt the cathedral.

(Below) King Cnut (1016–1035) is blessed by Christ as he presents a cross to a church. Like earlier English kings, William believed that God had chosen him to rule.

The last major threat to William's authority came in 1071, in the Fens of East Anglia. Supported by a Danish army, Earl Morcar and a Saxon lord called Hereward the Wake rebelled against Norman rule. William swiftly surrounded their camp on the lonely Isle of Ely. Then his soldiers built a **causeway** across the marshy fenland, marched across and defeated them. Many of the rebels were killed. Others were blinded or had their legs cut off as a punishment. From this time onwards, there was no serious opposition to William, and he spent most of his reign in Normandy.

William's success in ruling his new kingdom depended at first on his own skills as a military leader. But to control the country when the army was not available, he built castles. Every major town and city in England had a castle built at its centre. Where there were no hilltops, artificial mounds were built up. These gave the castles a view of the surrounding countryside and also made them hard to attack. At Norwich, for example, over forty Saxon houses and churches were destroyed to make space for the castle. A hundred or more soldiers were stationed there, watching over the city in case of trouble. These castles were an unwelcome reminder to the English that they were now the subjects of a Norman king.

The chamber block of Chepstow Castle in Gwent, Wales. William Fitz Osbern, one of William's most powerful lords, built this castle to protect England against Welsh attacks.

The King of England

WILLIAM · CONQVEROR ·

We do not know what William looked like. Here, an unknown sixteenth-century artist painted him as a king of his own day.

It is hard to know exactly what William was like. He left no writings. Indeed, since he could not write, he had to 'sign' documents using a cross as his mark. A **scribe** then wrote his name next to it. Those who wrote about William in his own day, such as his **biographer**, William of Poitiers, or the writer, Orderic Vitalis, were more interested in his actions than his personality.

All records agree that William was an exceptionally tall and powerful man. His tomb has been destroyed, but scientists have studied a thigh bone which survives from his body. They calculate that he was at least 1.75 metres tall – very large for that time.

Hunting animals was a popular way to practise horse skills. This scene from the Bayeux Tapestry shows King Harold hunting with a hawk and hounds.

Norman writers said that William had a loud, rough voice and that in later life he grew fat. He was famous for his stern and ferocious expression. According to the **chronicler**, William of Malmesbury, his shoulders were so strong that he could draw a bow that other men could not even bend, and fire it while **spurring** on his horse.

From childhood, William was very fond of hunting. He hunted animals not just for sport and food, but as training for war. He had sixty villages destroyed to create the New Forest for hunting in. Anyone who stole game from royal lands had their hands cut off. William must have spent much of his life on horseback, travelling, hunting and fighting.

The New Forest today. It was cleared of houses on William's orders. Many people blamed him for putting his sport before their livelihood.

William's cruelty was legendary, even though he lived in a cruel age. Most people expected their lives to be short and often painful. However, people who helped William had nothing to fear. Those who opposed him sometimes suffered horrible punishments.

Perhaps William's brutal methods were necessary for his success. But he knew that they were wrong in God's eyes. He was terrified that when he died he would be punished in Hell for his sins. Throughout his life, William took his duties as a Christian very seriously. Every morning, he attended Mass. Priests accompanied him everywhere, and he had chapels built in all his castles.

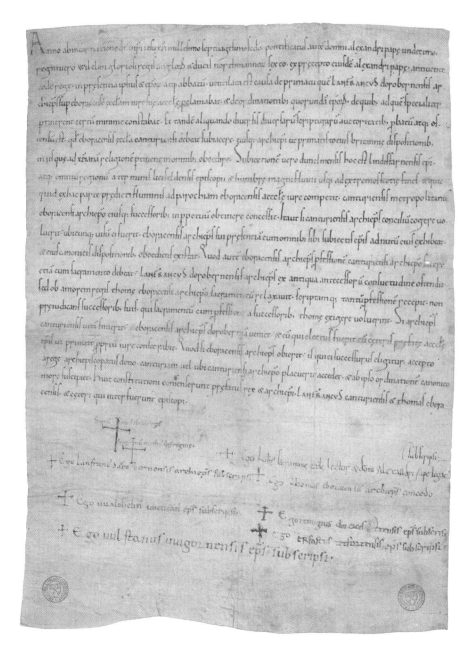

William could not read or write. To sign documents he made a cross mark. The first two crosses here are those of William and Queen Matilda.

The gateway to Battle Abbey. William founded this monastery, hoping to gain God's forgiveness for the sins of the Battle of Hastings.

To make up for his sins, William was very generous to the Church. In his early years as Duke, he founded the beautiful church of St Stephen in Caen. After the conquest of England, he gave money to build an abbey on the site of the Battle of Hastings. You can still see the ruins today – it is called Battle Abbey. He told the builders to put the main altar in the exact spot where King Harold had been killed. Every day, the monks had to pray that God would forgive William for the sins of the battle. He even ordered his soldiers to do a year's **penance** for the people they had killed.

A silver penny showing King William I. Coins were an important way of telling people who was the ruler.

This page from a Norman book shows the Norman kings William I, William II, Henry I and Stephen English. The artist wanted us to think that they were holy men, so he showed them holding churches.

William provided land and property for church buildings. Norman architects and masons helped to rebuild the old Saxon churches in the Norman style. William also brought over many monks, nuns, bishops and priests from France. One of these was his friend, the great scholar Lanfranc, who became Archbishop of Canterbury. With William's help, Lanfranc reorganized the English Church.

William had high standards of behaviour. He did not allow his followers to eat too much, get drunk, or grow long hair which was the English fashion.

Some time between 1049 and 1053, William had married Matilda, the daughter of the ruler of Flanders. This won him the support of other powerful royal families. William and Matilda had a deep love for each other. Though they were often apart, they always remained faithful. After the conquest of England, William relied heavily on his own family to govern his lands. Matilda took charge of Normandy while William was in England, and when he was in Normandy, England was governed by his half-brother Odo.

Matilda and William had nine children – five daughters and four sons. Cecilia, their eldest daughter, became a famous nun. The other daughters married princes or lords. Their son, Richard, was killed in a hunting accident. Of their other sons, William and Henry later became kings of England. Robert, the eldest, fell out with his father, but became Duke of Normandy after his death.

Archbishop Lanfranc. Under his leadership, the English Church became famous for its learning as well as its wealth.

St John's Chapel in the Tower of London. This was one of William's private churches where he regularly heard Mass.

'Peace of a Kind'

IMPORTANT DATES

1075 *Revolt of Earls Roger and Ralph.*

1077–80 *William quarrels with his son Robert.*

1081 *Robert defeats the Scots and founds Newcastle.*

1086 Domesday Book *is compiled.*

William sails for Normandy.

1087 *William dies and is buried in Caen.*

The first years of William's reign were often confused and bloody. But in 1073, Archbishop Lanfranc wrote to the Pope saying, 'While the King lives we have peace of a kind.' The worst was over. From then on, William spent most of his time in Normandy. Peace and order returned to England.

But the king's troubles were never quite over. At a wedding feast in Norwich, two Norman lords, Ralph and Roger, hatched a plot to overthrow him. They were angry with William for sending judges to hold courts on their lands. William was in Normandy, so Odo led an army against the rebels. Earl Ralph held Norwich Castle against the king's troops, but then fled, leaving his wife Emma to face defeat.

William's castle at Norwich was a wooden building perched on top of a steep mound. It was rebuilt shortly after his death using stone from Normandy.

Robert, William's eldest son. He became Duke of Normandy on William's death in 1087. His tomb is in Gloucester Cathedral.

Back in Normandy, trouble now came from William's oldest son Robert. With William as King of England, Robert wanted to be Duke of Normandy. William refused. Robert then raised an army and attacked Norman towns. At Gerberoi, father and son fought each other until Robert wounded William in the hand. Eventually, in 1080, they made peace. William agreed that Robert could be Duke – after his death.

Newcastle-upon-Tyne today. The 'new castle' here was built to protect Norman England against the Scots.

The following year, William and Robert were back in England. Robert now led an army north to put a stop to raids from the Scots. Robert's castle in Northumberland is now the site of Newcastle-upon-Tyne.

To rule England well, William needed to know who owned what, which lands had recently changed hands and how much tax people could pay. He ordered a detailed **survey** to be carried out in 1086. People called it the *Domesday Book*, because it seemed like the Last Judgement spoken of in the Bible ('dom' or 'doom' is the old English word for judgement).

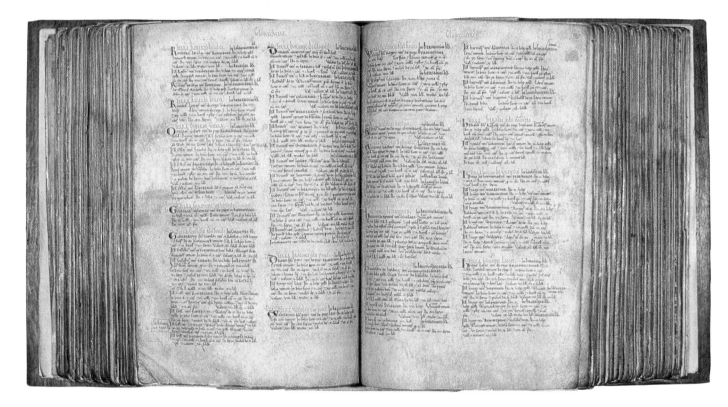

One of the volumes of the Domesday Book. The survey was resented by the English. They thought that they would pay higher taxes because the survey would show how much they could afford to pay.

Men travelled all over the country, asking who had owned the land and property in 1066 and in 1086. They counted the peasants, animals, ploughs, mills and even fish ponds. This information was recorded and compiled into two huge books. It was the most detailed survey carried out in medieval times.

William sailed for Normandy in 1086. He never returned. By July 1087, he was sixty years old (a great age then). Troubled by raids from France, he unwisely led an attack on the French town of Mantes. William's horse stumbled. He was thrown against the iron **pommel** of his saddle and was fatally injured in the stomach. As William lay dying, he sent his favourite son William Rufus to claim the crown of England.

William's body was shipped around the coast to Caen and buried in the abbey church of St Stephen. But, the tomb was too small, and his body split open as it was being squeezed into the narrow grave. Most people fled from the church, as they had done at his coronation. It was an undignified end for such a remarkable man.

(Above) Durham Cathedral, begun in 1093. It was one of the first English churches built in the round-arched Norman style.

The site of William's tomb in the abbey church which he founded in Caen, in Normandy.

Glossary

ancestors Members of a family, who lived long ago.

archers Soldiers who are armed with bows and arrows.

biographer The author of someone's life story.

causeway A raised path crossing water, marshland or sand.

cavalry Soldiers who fight on horseback.

chronicler Someone who records historical events in the order that they happened.

congregation A group of people who attend a church service.

conquests Lands that are captured in battles or wars.

descendants Later generations of a family which can be traced back.

duke An important lord or ruler.

elected Chosen to rule or govern.

fleet A group of ships.

illegitimate Someone whose parents are not married.

legends Stories about things which happened long ago. Most legends are not true.

oath A promise.

penance Doing good deeds to make up for bad ones.

pilgrimage A special journey made to a holy place.

pommel A round knob that was found on the front of a saddle.

Pope The head of the Roman Catholic Church.

rebel Someone who decides not to obey the people in power.

scribe Someone who is employed to write things down.

spurring Urging a horse to move on more quickly.

status Position in society.

steward Someone who was in charge of a lord's household.

survey An investigation, questioning people about a particular subject.

tanner A person who makes raw animal skins into leather.

territory Lands ruled.

Vikings Invaders and settlers who came to England from Denmark, Norway and Sweden during the eighth and eleventh centuries.

Further Information

Books to Read

History in Evidence – Norman Britain by T. D. Triggs (Wayland, 1990)
Norman Castles by G. Rickard (Wayland, 1989)
Norman Invaders and Settlers by T. D. Triggs (Wayland, 1992)
The Normans by P. Rooke (Macdonald, 1987)
Young Researcher – The Normans by H.M. Martell (Heinemann, 1992)

Places to Visit

In France:

Abbey of St Stephen, Caen.
This great church was founded by William and was his burial place.

Bayeux Cathedral, Bayeux.
A richly decorated Norman church, built for William's half-brother Odo.

Falaise Castle, Falaise.
An early twelfth-century stone castle that was built on the site of William's birthplace.

Tapestry Museum, Bayeux.
Contains the original Bayeux Tapestry, with an English language audio guide.

In Britain:

Battle, Sussex.
The site of the Battle of Hastings, with a battlefield walk, exhibition and the remains of William's Battle Abbey. Battle Museum has a copy of the Bayeux Tapestry.

British Museum, London.
See the *Domesday Book* and other documents and objects from William's reign.

Castle Museum, Colchester, Essex.
A Norman building with interactive displays about Norman life.

Chepstow Castle, Wales.
One of the first stone Norman castles, begun by William FitzOsbern in 1067.

Durham Castle and Cathedral, Durham.
Perhaps the finest Norman building in England.

Ely, Cambridgeshire.
The location of Hereward's revolt, with a Norman castle mound and a magnificent cathedral begun soon after William's death.

The Tower of London, London.
The strongest Norman castle, begun in William's lifetime, which contains his private chapel of St. John.

Index

Figures in **bold** refer to illustrations. Glossary entries are shown by the letter g.